THE A.I. HUSTLE

MASTERING DIGITAL AUTOMATION AND PASSIVE INCOME

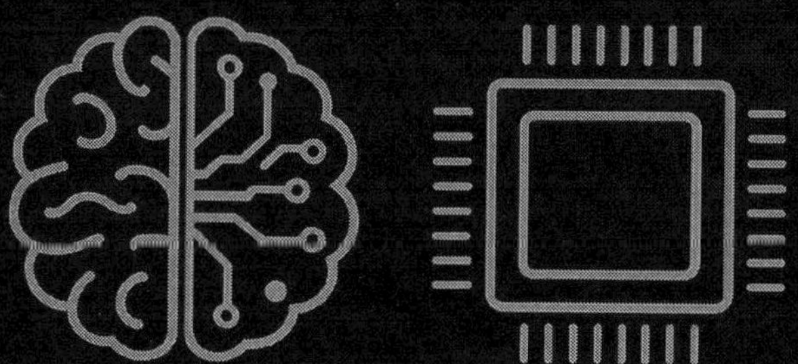

The A.I Hustle

"Your daily assistant for turning dreams into reality."

Introduction: The Power Shift Begins

To those who refuse to remain ordinary,

You are entering a new arena — one not built by governments or institutions, but by code, creativity, and quiet revolutions happening on laptops around the world. The rules have changed. Power no longer belongs solely to the wealthy or the well-connected. It now lies in the hands of those who can harness information and technology — and wield it with intention.

The A.I. Hustle is not merely a book. It is a strategy. A compass for those who sense a shift in the air but are unsure how to act. We stand at the edge of a technological frontier where artificial intelligence is no longer science fiction — it is the infrastructure of tomorrow's wealth, influence, and innovation.

This series exists to dismantle the illusion that A.I. is only for the elite. The truth is far more empowering: it is for the self-taught, the underdog, the misunderstood visionary. It is for you.

Fear and confusion are the enemies of progress. You may feel intimidated by this technology, unsure of where to begin or if it's even worth your time. That is no accident — systems were designed to keep the masses unaware of the tools that can free them. This book aims to expose that veil and hand you the tools directly.

Here, A.I. becomes more than software. It becomes your strategist, your silent partner, your amplifier. Whether you seek freedom from financial struggle, elevation in your business, or the realization of a vision you've carried in secret — you now have a means.

Use this book as your map. Not to follow, but to adapt. The journey to mastery begins with awareness. The A.I. revolution is already underway. The question is — will you observe it from the sidelines, or will you position yourself to win?

Welcome to *The A.I. Hustle* — the new playbook for those who refuse to play by old rules.

Table of Contents

12. 💎 **Bonus Chapter (Exclusive Access): The 90-Day Execution Plan + Entry to The Inner Circle**
    Unlock this chapter by joining the official A.I. Hustle Discord – featuring tools, community, and a private A.I. chatbot built to support your journey to financial independence.

Chapter One: The New Currency — Understanding A.I. in the Age of Leverage

"Power is not given. It is taken — by those who see opportunity before it becomes obvious."

The rules of the economy have changed. But like all true revolutions, it didn't start with a declaration. It started in silence — behind screens, in basements, in forgotten corners of the internet. While the world argued over politics and pandemics, a new power was quietly taking root.

Artificial Intelligence — to the untrained mind, it sounds like some distant, sterile technology meant for Silicon Valley geniuses or billion-dollar enterprises. But the truth is far more dangerous — and far more liberating. A.I. is not just for coders. It is for the hustler. The dreamer. The rebel who's tired of asking for permission to succeed.

The Great Shift: From Labor to Leverage

For centuries, the currency of success was sweat. You clocked in, you worked long, you hoped someone noticed. But today, leverage is the new sweat. One person with a laptop and the right tools can outperform an entire team trapped in outdated systems.

Consider this: a single mother in Atlanta creates a children's book using A.I. art tools and sells it online. Within months, she replaces her job. A teenager in the Philippines uses ChatGPT to build marketing copy for e-commerce stores and is earning more than college graduates. These aren't stories of luck — they are stories of **leverage**.

What used to require degrees, gatekeepers, or thousands in startup capital, now only requires knowledge — and boldness. That's the new game. And it's being played whether you're in or not.

A.I. as an Equalizer

In every era, technology creates two classes of people: **the builders** and **the spectators**. The builders learn just enough to create something. The spectators wait for someone else to figure it out and feed it to them. And while they wait, the world moves on.

A.I. is your chance to become a builder — even if you've never written a line of code, even if you dropped out, even if your past is littered with failures.

It is your assistant, your strategist, your silent partner.

It doesn't complain. It doesn't sleep. It doesn't make excuses.

And in the hands of someone who understands value, it can unlock income streams, automate time-wasting tasks, and make your smallest ideas feel like empire blueprints.

Real Life: A Hustler's Choice

You may have grown up in an environment where options were limited. Maybe you've worked jobs that drained your spirit. Maybe you've been told that success has a certain look, a certain pedigree. Here's the truth: A.I. doesn't care where you're from. It doesn't care if you have a criminal record or a 4.0 GPA. It only amplifies what you feed it.

Garbage in, garbage out.

Strategy in, freedom out.

You now live in a world where your ideas, when paired with the right tools, can outperform legacy institutions. Your edge is not how hard you work — it's how smart and fast you execute.

The Mindset Shift

Before we go deeper into tools, techniques, and business models, you must first shift your mindset. A.I. is not here to do the work for you. It is here to multiply your efforts. It is not a magic wand — it is a weapon. Like any weapon, it can be used recklessly or masterfully.

This book exists to teach you mastery.

The financially free in this era will be those who learned how to command the machine — not fear it. Those who use A.I. to solve problems for others, build scalable systems, and free up their own time are not just making money — they are buying back their lives.

This is not just a hustle. This is a revolution in disguise.

Coming Up: In Chapter Two, we'll dive into *Digital Identity* — how to craft an online presence that speaks for you 24/7 and opens doors before you knock.

Chapter Two: Digital Identity — Crafting Your Online Presence with Precision

"In the modern world, your digital identity speaks before you enter the room — and echoes long after you leave."

In ancient times, power came from bloodlines, land, and family names. Then it came from capital and connections. But today, your **digital identity** is your reputation, your portfolio, your resume, and your storefront — all at once.

In the A.I. era, you are not simply building a presence — you're building **perception**. And perception, when executed with precision, is more powerful than any pitch.

You Are Who the Internet Says You Are

Pause and ask yourself: if a stranger Googled your name right now, what would they find?

If your name is attached to nothing, you are essentially invisible. In a world that operates through screens, being invisible is financial suicide. You could have the skills. The heart. The hustle. But if your **digital reflection** doesn't match your **real-life value**, the world won't pay attention.

You must **curate the narrative**.

Because if you don't, the world will do it for you — and they'll usually get it wrong.

The Digital Storefront: Social Media as Strategic Real Estate

Think of your Instagram, your LinkedIn, your YouTube channel not as social platforms — but as **real estate** in the attention economy. Every post, every caption, every reel is either building equity in your brand or devaluing it.

Let me give you a real-life scenario:

There's a young man from Houston who used to rap, hustle, and barely post online. In 2022, he learned how to use A.I. to schedule content, clean up his captions, and optimize his hashtags. Within 6 months, he went from 1,200 followers to 40,000 — but more importantly, he started getting paid. Artists were booking him for consultations. Labels were asking him how he was doing it.

He didn't get a new talent. He got a new **strategy**.

With A.I., you don't need to be a marketing expert. Tools now exist that help you write bios, plan content calendars, and even auto-generate engagement scripts. You're no longer waiting on a team. You're building yourself into one.

The Profile Audit: Commanding Presence

Here's a quick digital identity checklist. If you're missing any of these, you're leaving opportunity on the table:

- A clear and strategic **bio** that communicates your value in one sentence.
- A **professional photo** (or a stylized brand image) that reflects your tone.
- A link-in-bio tool that leads visitors to your offer, service, or product.
- At least 3 high-quality content posts that demonstrate **expertise or authenticity**.
- Highlights or pinned posts that answer the question: *"Why should I follow or trust you?"*

Every platform is a funnel. Every piece of content is either attracting or repelling opportunity.

Building Digital Trust Through Consistency

Powerful brands aren't built in one viral moment. They are built through consistent, clear messaging. A.I. can help you pre-plan your posting schedule, analyze trends, and even respond to comments like a human. But none of that matters if you lack clarity in your identity.

Are you here to educate? Inspire? Sell? Entertain? Pick a lane. Own it. Then build around it.

Even if you pivot later, start somewhere **bold and specific**.

"He who masters visibility, masters attention. He who masters attention, writes his own check."

Chapter Three: Tools of the Trade — Building with A.I. as Your Silent Partner

"A man with tools is dangerous. A man who masters them becomes unstoppable."

Every era had its power tools: the printing press, the steam engine, the computer. In our era, it is artificial intelligence. But the real power isn't in having the tools — it's in how you use them. **A.I. is only as powerful as the mind commanding it.**

This chapter isn't just about listing apps. It's about understanding how to build your *digital empire* with systems that never sleep, never get tired, and scale with you.

The Myth of Complexity

Most people are intimidated by A.I. because they've been lied to.

They think it's reserved for engineers or computer scientists. That belief is not just false — it's dangerous. It keeps dreamers stuck. It keeps hustlers dependent. It keeps underdogs from becoming kings.

The truth? Most A.I. tools are *plug and play*. What took agencies weeks now takes you minutes. What cost five figures can be done for $20/month — or free. The gatekeepers are panicking for a reason.

You don't need permission anymore.

You need **direction**.

Section I: Your Daily Operator – ChatGPT (or Claude, Gemini, etc.)

This is your **thinking assistant** — your planner, your ghostwriter, your research analyst, and even your customer service agent. It's not just for answering questions; it's for structuring your life.

Examples:

- Write email pitches to brands.
- Draft legal disclaimers for your website.
- Create a 30-day content calendar based on your niche.
- Build an entire course outline in 3 minutes.

Prompt like a boss, and you'll get results like a strategist. Lazy prompts = basic output.

Section II: Visual Empire – Midjourney & Canva

Humans are visual creatures. You can have the dopest idea in the world — if it looks sloppy, it gets ignored. Period.

Use Midjourney (advanced) for:

- Album covers
- Book illustrations
- Unique product packaging

Use Canva (accessible) for:

- Flyers
- Website banners
- Instagram carousels
- Business cards

Design is no longer a barrier. You are now your own creative team.

Section III: Automation = Freedom – Zapier, Make, & Notion AI

Imagine setting up a system once — and it handles business while you sleep.

Zapier/Make:

- Auto-send welcome emails when someone joins your list.
- Post new content across platforms with one action.
- Get notified when someone makes a purchase, fills out a form, or subscribes.

Notion AI:

- Plan out your week, goals, or product roadmap with assisted intelligence.
- Summarize notes and create task lists instantly.
- Track customer feedback, brand goals, and content calendars in one digital workspace.

Automation doesn't make you lazy — it makes you scalable.

Section IV: Voice & Video – ElevenLabs, Descript, CapCut

Your content should live in multiple formats. Repurpose like a strategist.

Descript:

- Edit video like text.
- Remove “ums” and filler words in seconds.
- Generate captions automatically.

ElevenLabs:

- Clone your voice and narrate articles, eBooks, or ads.

CapCut (free + mobile):

- Auto-cut reels, add trending sounds, and generate subtitles for short-form videos.

You don’t need a studio anymore — just a smartphone and skill.

The Rule of Tools

Here’s a truth many won’t tell you:

It’s not about how many tools you have. It’s about how you use the **few that match your vision.**

Start simple. Master the fundamentals. Then expand.

Don't chase hype — chase mastery.

Up Next: In Chapter Four, we dive deep into **Monetizing the Machine** — how to use these tools to actually make money, build offers, and escape the trap of always trading time for cash.

Chapter Four: Monetizing the Machine — Turning A.I. Into Income

"Power unused is power wasted. A tool not turned into profit is just digital decoration."

You've explored the tools. You've started crafting your identity. But now it's time to shift the lens from creation to **conversion** — from building to **earning**.

This chapter is your pivot point — where ambition becomes action. A.I. isn't just here to make life easier. It's here to **make life richer**, if you know how to turn its capabilities into capital.

Why Most People Stay Broke in a Digital Gold Rush

Let's be real: the internet is flooded with creators, sellers, influencers — and most are broke.

Why?

Because they lead with attention, not **value**. They chase likes, not **leverage**. They build traffic without understanding what to do with it.

A.I. flips the game. It allows you to create high-value products, systems, and services in a fraction of the time — without the overhead. But only if you treat it like a partner, not a toy.

Strategy 1: Digital Products – Selling Knowledge, Not Time

You have something you know that someone else wants to learn.

A.I. can help you:

- Outline and write an eBook in days, not months.
- Build an online course from scratch, complete with modules, scripts, and slides.
- Create a paid newsletter that runs on autopilot.

Case Study:
A single mother in Atlanta used ChatGPT to ghostwrite an eBook on parenting toddlers. She sold it for $9.99. With no prior audience, she made $1,300 in her first 30 days. Her secret? She posted in parenting Facebook groups and offered real solutions. She never touched design — Canva and ChatGPT handled it all.

Lesson: Don't sell dreams. Sell **solutions**. Use A.I. to build once, sell forever.

Strategy 2: Freelancing + A.I. = Elite Services at Scale

People will always pay to have things done for them.

A.I. allows you to:

- Offer content writing, branding, and copy services.
- Build business plans, pitch decks, or product descriptions.
- Translate content, improve resumes, or analyze data — fast.

Real Game: You don't have to do it all. Use ChatGPT or other models as your backend assistant. You're not cheating. You're **scaling**.

Offer real services, charge reasonable rates, and deliver faster than your competitors. That's how you win repeat business.

Strategy 3: Automation Agency – The "Invisible" Income

Small businesses are behind. They still send invoices manually, schedule social media by hand, and forget to follow up with leads.

You can fix that — and get paid well to do it.

What You Can Offer:

- Automate their emails, texts, or onboarding sequences.
- Set up appointment booking flows.
- Use Zapier/Make to build systems they didn't even know were possible.

You don't have to be a tech expert. Use what you've learned and let A.I. guide the build.

Clients don't care how you do it. They care that it **works**.

Strategy 4: Brand Building + Affiliate Marketing

If you're not ready to sell your own products, promote someone else's — and get paid every time they make a sale.

You can:

- Use A.I. to write product reviews.
- Create niche-specific TikToks or YouTube Shorts.
- Set up auto-reply funnels that lead people to purchase links.

You become the middleman — and the commission flows in.

The Truth About Earning with A.I.

Let's clear the air: **This isn't magic.**
You still need discipline. You still need to test. You still need to show up.

But the edge A.I. gives you is **speed**.
Precision.
Endless creation with minimal burnout.

The difference between surviving and scaling? The one who **executes faster** wins.

"Money flows to speed, skill, and systems. A.I. gives you all three."

Chapter Five: Personalization at Scale — How to Build Loyalty in a Cold World

"People don't buy products. They buy belief, identity, and trust."

In an era flooded with automation and mass production, the currency of trust has never been more valuable — or more scarce. Every brand screams. Every ad begs. Every influencer performs.

So how do you cut through the noise?

You stop treating people like numbers.

You use **A.I. to scale personalization** — to build intimacy in a digital world where most are chasing volume instead of value.

The Illusion of Automation

Most people think automation means emotionless. Cold. Robotic. But that's because they use tools **without intention**.

They copy-paste. They blast messages. They automate junk — and call it marketing.

But the true master? He builds systems that feel **human**.

He uses A.I. to write like a friend, reply like a partner, and sell like a surgeon.

System 1: Email with Empathy – Using A.I. for Warm Communication

Stop sending emails that sound like corporate ads. Start sending messages that feel like letters from a mentor, a partner, a motivator.

ChatGPT + Email Framework = Personal Gold

Use A.I. to:

- Segment your list based on actions and behavior.
- Write weekly emails that feel **crafted** for the reader.
- Inject personality, story, and subtle persuasion.

Example Prompt:

"Write a 3-part email sequence for new subscribers who joined my AI hustle newsletter. Tone: inspiring, motivational, personal — like a coach who knows they've got potential."

Test. Refine. Then automate the delivery — not the heart.

System 2: Chatbots That Feel Like Humans

Imagine a chatbot that doesn't just answer questions — it understands your brand voice, your mission, and your ideal customer's mindset.

What You Can Do:

- Train a chatbot on your brand's tone, values, and offer stack.
- Answer questions in real-time about your services, prices, and products.
- Guide new visitors through a personalized journey (like a digital concierge).

You're not just saving time. You're building trust **while you sleep.**

System 3: Personalized Offers Based on Behavior

Using platforms like **ManyChat, Intercom, or MailerLite**, you can:

- Send different offers based on user clicks, quiz results, or time spent on your site.
- Automatically follow up on abandoned carts with empathetic reminders.
- Offer loyalty discounts based on past purchases or engagement.

Use A.I. to observe, predict, and respond. That's what personalization is about — not guessing, but knowing.

The Power of Story-Driven Funnels

Every successful brand has one thing in common: **a clear story**.

Your audience isn't just buying access to your tools.
They're buying access to your **journey**. Your wins. Your scars. Your vision.

Craft your funnel like a documentary, not a pitch deck.

A.I. can help you:

- Write your origin story in your voice.
- Build landing pages with copy that pulls people in.
- Test variations of your message and see what sticks.

People crave authenticity. Use the machine to amplify it — not replace it.

Final Insight: The Paradox of Scale

When you scale without personalization, you lose trust.

When you personalize without systems, you burn out.

But when you blend the two — personalization at scale — you become **untouchable**.

"A king who speaks to his people, not at them, rules longer."

Chapter Six: Building an Ecosystem — From Side Hustle to Digital Empire

"The difference between a hustler and a ruler is architecture. One survives. The other builds."

You've learned how to use A.I. to earn. You've used it to scale, automate, and connect. But true wealth — the kind that frees you — requires more than just money. It requires **structure**.

This chapter is your blueprint for building a **self-sustaining ecosystem**, where every piece of your effort feeds the next. A side hustle becomes a brand. A brand becomes a business. And the business becomes a **movement**.

What Is a Digital Ecosystem?

An ecosystem is a **circle** — not a straight line.

It's not "post content → get paid → repeat."

It's:

1. **Create Value**
2. **Capture Attention**
3. **Convert Loyalty into Revenue**
4. **Reinvest into Content, Tools, and Community**
5. **Repeat with Momentum**

This is the game the wealthy play. They don't chase one-off wins. They build **compounding machines**.

The Core Components of Your A.I. Empire

1. The Front End: Discovery

This is where people find you. Use A.I. to fuel:

- YouTube videos with strong hooks and storytelling.
- TikTok clips with captions and trend awareness.
- Blog posts or tweets written for SEO and virality.

Each piece is bait — but it must be real.
Authenticity is your magnet. Consistency is your weapon.

2. The Funnel: Connection

A stranger becomes a supporter through experience. Use A.I. to:

- Design funnels that greet, educate, and guide.
- Build welcome sequences that introduce your story.
- Recommend next steps based on interest and interaction.

3. The Offer: Monetization

Your content earns trust. Your offer earns income.

- A.I.-written courses, eBooks, templates, or subscriptions.
- Consultation bookings automated by calendar flows.
- Memberships, Discord access, coaching — the value ladder.

The trick? Each offer solves a problem deeper than the last.

4. The Back End: Automation & Scale

Now you're busy. But busy isn't the goal — **freedom** is.

- Automate emails, course delivery, content scheduling.
- Use Zapier, Notion, or Airtable to centralize operations.
- Build a small VA team and train them with A.I.-generated SOPs (Standard Operating Procedures).

Real-Life Blueprint: From Hustle to Empire

Scenario:

Let's say you start a brand teaching beginners how to use A.I. for marketing.

Month 1–2:

- Write a free guide using ChatGPT.
- Offer it in exchange for email signups.
- Post 3–5x weekly with tips, breakdowns, and behind-the-scenes content.

Month 3–4:

- Release a $17 eBook and a $97 mini-course.
- Set up automated email sequences with weekly value drops.
- Build a Discord server for paying members.

Month 5–6:

- Add 1-on-1 coaching at $150/session.
- Begin affiliate marketing for tools you use.

- Release a $297 “Launch Accelerator” bundle with ChatGPT scripts, templates, and workflows.

In 6 months, what started as a hustle becomes a **machine**.

Rule of the Digital Kingdom: Reinvest Power

Each win must fuel the next:

- Use income to pay for better systems and sharper design.
- Use feedback to improve your funnel and offers.
- Use time saved to create deeper, richer content.

Power ignored becomes power lost.

"The wise ruler invests in his castle, not just his crown."

Chapter Six: Building an Ecosystem — From Side Hustle to Digital Empire

"The difference between a hustler and a ruler is architecture. One survives. The other builds."

You've learned how to use A.I. to earn. You've used it to scale, automate, and connect. But true wealth — the kind that frees you — requires more than just money. It requires **structure**.

This chapter is your blueprint for building a **self-sustaining ecosystem**, where every piece of your effort feeds the next. A side hustle becomes a brand. A brand becomes a business. And the business becomes a **movement**.

What Is a Digital Ecosystem?

An ecosystem is a **circle** — not a straight line.

It's not "post content → get paid → repeat."

It's:

1. **Create Value**
2. **Capture Attention**
3. **Convert Loyalty into Revenue**
4. **Reinvest into Content, Tools, and Community**
5. **Repeat with Momentum**

This is the game the wealthy play. They don't chase one-off wins. They build **compounding machines**.

The Core Components of Your A.I. Empire

1. The Front End: Discovery

This is where people find you. Use A.I. to fuel:

- YouTube videos with strong hooks and storytelling.
- TikTok clips with captions and trend awareness.
- Blog posts or tweets written for SEO and virality.

Each piece is bait — but it must be real.
Authenticity is your magnet. Consistency is your weapon.

2. The Funnel: Connection

A stranger becomes a supporter through experience. Use A.I. to:

- Design funnels that greet, educate, and guide.
- Build welcome sequences that introduce your story.
- Recommend next steps based on interest and interaction.

3. The Offer: Monetization

Your content earns trust. Your offer earns income.

- A.I.-written courses, eBooks, templates, or subscriptions.
- Consultation bookings automated by calendar flows.
- Memberships, Discord access, coaching — the value ladder.

The trick? Each offer solves a problem deeper than the last.

4. The Back End: Automation & Scale

Now you're busy. But busy isn't the goal — **freedom** is.

- Automate emails, course delivery, content scheduling.
- Use Zapier, Notion, or Airtable to centralize operations.
- Build a small VA team and train them with A.I.-generated SOPs (Standard Operating Procedures).

Real-Life Blueprint: From Hustle to Empire

Scenario:

Let's say you start a brand teaching beginners how to use A.I. for marketing.

Month 1–2:

- Write a free guide using ChatGPT.
- Offer it in exchange for email signups.
- Post 3–5x weekly with tips, breakdowns, and behind-the-scenes content.

Month 3–4:

- Release a $17 eBook and a $97 mini-course.
- Set up automated email sequences with weekly value drops.
- Build a Discord server for paying members.

Month 5–6:

- Add 1-on-1 coaching at $150/session.
- Begin affiliate marketing for tools you use.

- Release a $297 “Launch Accelerator” bundle with ChatGPT scripts, templates, and workflows.

In 6 months, what started as a hustle becomes a **machine**.

Rule of the Digital Kingdom: Reinvest Power

Each win must fuel the next:

- Use income to pay for better systems and sharper design.
- Use feedback to improve your funnel and offers.
- Use time saved to create deeper, richer content.

Power ignored becomes power lost.

"The wise ruler invests in his castle, not just his crown."

Chapter Seven: Overcoming Resistance — The Inner Game of the A.I. Hustler

"Before a man conquers the world, he must conquer his own hesitation."

The tools are here. The playbook is in your hands. But there's a battle that no software can fight for you — the one inside your own mind.

This chapter is about resistance — the invisible force that keeps most people **almost successful**, **almost ready**, and **almost great**.

You've felt it before.

That voice that says:

"You're not ready."
"What if they laugh?"
"What if this fails?"

But here's the truth: that voice is not your enemy. It's your **test**.

The Psychology of Delay

Every A.I. hustler begins with excitement. You see the possibilities. You feel the spark. But then, **you hesitate.**

Why?

Because success demands exposure. Visibility. Risk. Accountability.

Most people would rather fantasize about success than actually do the work, because **dreams are safe — results are proof**.

"Better to never try, than to try and fail."
That's the lie resistance tells you.

But the real tragedy?
Not failing.
Regretting you never started.

Resistance Has Many Disguises

- **Perfectionism:** "It's not ready yet."
- **Overthinking:** "What's the best angle?"
- **Comparison:** "Others are better than me."
- **Burnout:** "Maybe I'll wait until next month."
- **Imposter Syndrome:** "Who am I to teach this?"

Resistance will use your voice to convince you to stay small.

But every chapter you write, every video you post, every system you launch — you chip away at the lie.

Real-Life Parallel: The Boxer and the Bell

Imagine a young fighter. Gifted. Trained. Hungry.

But every time the bell rings, he freezes. Not because he can't fight — but because he's afraid of what happens if he **loses** in front of everyone.

So he keeps training. Keeps preparing. **Never enters the ring.**

Many talented people die with their potential locked inside them because they never rang their own bell.

You must choose the bell over the bag.

Tools to Beat Resistance — Built With A.I.

Here's how to use technology to discipline the mind:

1. A.I. Journaling for Clarity
Use ChatGPT or Notion to reflect:

"Today, I felt resistance when ____. What triggered it? How can I reframe it?"

2. Daily Micro-Plans
Build daily 3-task prompts:

"What 3 moves today will move me forward, no matter how small?"

3. Voice Notes to Self
Record affirmations or action reviews. Use ElevenLabs or ChatGPT's voice integration to talk to your future self.

4. Create a Self-Accountability Bot
Use a simple chatbot that checks in every day:

"Did you create today or consume?"
"Did you build or scroll?"

What Winners Know

Success is not about being fearless. It's about knowing that fear is part of the journey — and still walking through the fire.

A.I. can give you the script.
The tools.
The schedule.
But **you** have to show up.

Not just once — **every damn day**.

"Discipline is the bridge between talent and legacy."

Final Thought: Make Resistance Work for You

Let fear signal where to go.
Let doubt remind you that you care.
Let hesitation become the trigger to act, not retreat.

You weren't given this book to read passively.
You were given this because you're meant to build, teach, lead, and evolve.

Turn resistance into ritual.

Chapter Eight: Case Studies — Real People, Real Plays, Real Results

"Don't just tell me it works. Show me the receipts."

Every movement needs evidence. Every system, validation.
This chapter reveals **living examples** of everyday people who used A.I. to elevate, pivot, and **profit** — without fame, connections, or a tech degree.

These are not fairy tales. These are **frameworks in action.**

Case Study 1: The Single Mom Turned Digital Coach

Background:
Ashley, a 36-year-old mother of two, worked full-time at a call center. She had zero tech experience and thought A.I. was "some sci-fi stuff for rich people."

Play:

- Discovered ChatGPT on YouTube.
- Began journaling with it nightly to unpack her passion — helping people with relationship recovery.
- Used ChatGPT to write blog posts, create a free guide, and launch a TikTok channel.

Results:

- Within 90 days, 5K+ email subscribers.
- Sold her first eBook for $15 — made $7,800 in the first month.
- Launched a $97 mini-course — hit $21K by month five.

What Changed:
Ashley went from *"I'm not qualified"* to *"I control my income."*
A.I. didn't replace her — it **revealed her.**

Case Study 2: The Hustler Who Built a Niche Subscription Empire

Background:
Jay, 29, a former streetwear reseller from Atlanta. No college. Hustler by nature, scattered by default.

Play:

- Learned to use A.I. to write marketing emails, plan drops, and automate customer service.
- Used Midjourney to create exclusive digital clothing mockups and sell concepts before production.
- Built a Discord where fans paid $10/month to access early drops, style guides, and brand insights.

Results:

- Community grew to 1,700 members in 6 months.
- Launched a $49 digital fashion toolkit with ChatGPT prompts and design templates.
- Quit his 9–5 job. Bought his first studio space.

What Changed:
Jay stopped trying to do everything manually. He replaced chaos with a **system** — and the system printed money.

Case Study 3: The Former Inmate Turned Digital Architect

Background:
DeShawn, 34, served 4.5 years on a non-violent conspiracy charge. He got out with a vision and a chip on his shoulder — but no roadmap.

Play:

- Studied prompt engineering inside local libraries.
- Used A.I. to help artists write bios, plan releases, and structure deals.
- Built a private file-sharing network for music collaborations and began selling access to producers and managers.

Results:

- Made $2,000 in the first week just organizing beats and metadata with ChatGPT.
- Turned the service into a monthly subscription at $39/month.
- Helped three artists land licensing deals using A.I.-written pitch decks.

What Changed:
DeShawn refused to be defined by his past — and used A.I. to create a **new economy** around his talents.

Common Threads: What They All Did Right

1. **Started Small.**
   None of them waited to become "experts." They just started. A blog. A video. A template.

2. **Documented the Journey.**
   They didn't act like gurus — they invited people along for the ride.

3. **Created Feedback Loops.**
   They learned fast. Let the market guide them. Used A.I. to test, adapt, repeat.

4. **Built with Purpose.**
   This wasn't just about money. It was about freedom, healing, revenge, pride. That fire created **momentum.**

Your Case Study Is Next

What makes these stories powerful is not the numbers — it's the decisions.

The choice to act.
The choice to adapt.
The choice to evolve.

You are not behind.
You're right on time.

"Every empire begins with one tool, one mission, and one bold move."

Your name belongs in the next chapter of this series — but you have to **build it**.

Bonus Chapter: The Hidden Chamber — Discord Access & The A.I. Hustle Toolbox

"The difference between a reader and a builder… is access."
— *The A.I. Hustle Doctrine*

You've made it this far. You didn't just skim pages — you studied the blueprint.
Now, you unlock something most will never touch: ongoing support, real-time tools, and a private digital war room.

This is more than a book. It's a movement.

🔑 Welcome to the Discord: The Inner Circle

Your purchase grants you **exclusive access** to the private Discord server — the official home of the A.I. Hustlers.

This isn't just another forum. This is your command center, where knowledge becomes execution.

Inside, you'll find:

- 🧠 **The Prompt Lab:**
  A vault of daily-tested prompts to build your business, your brand, and your mindset.

- 💬 **Hustle Chatbot (Beta):**
  A custom-trained A.I. assistant built for this community — trained to help with niche research, business plans, writing, and tech walkthroughs.

- 🎥 **Live Build Sessions:**
  Weekly workshops where we create in real-time — websites, landing pages, ad scripts, brand strategies.

- 📁 **Template & Script Vault:**
  Downloadable A.I. email sequences, marketing campaigns, eBook structures, and digital product layouts.

- 📈 **Hustler Check-ins:**
  Subscription-based coaching and accountability. Not fluff. Not hype. Just straight strategy and support.

🛠 Why This Toolbox Is Priceless

Most people buy books, finish them, and go back to their old life. You? You're stepping into a system designed to grow with you.

Think of this as your living cheat code:

- Stuck on a digital product? Ask the bot.
- Need fresh content? Use the Prompt Lab.
- Want feedback? Jump into a live session.
- Hit a wall? DM the community.

No more guessing. No more isolation. Just execution with guidance.

🧾 How to Join

Verify Purchase
After buying this book, follow the link provided on the final page to access the Discord invite form.

Subscribe to Unlock Premium Tools
General access is free.
Premium tier (includes chatbot + live sessions) is subscription-based, offering monthly or yearly options to match your commitment.

Plug In, Level Up
Introduce yourself.
Share your mission.
Watch how fast your clarity compounds once you're inside the right circle.

Final Word to the Ambitious

This world doesn't reward the smartest. It rewards the most disciplined and plugged in.

You now have:

- The mindset
- The tools
- The plays
- The community

You're no longer alone on this journey.

"The future belongs to those who show up for it — daily, boldly, and without permission."

Join the A.I. Hustle Discord now: https://discord.gg/zkWAtXag

Made in the USA
Columbia, SC
27 June 2025

59940489R00024